Chess for Beginners

How to Win Almost Every Game with Proven Simple Tactics,

Proven Opening Strategies, and a Complete Knowledge of the

Rules and Pieces

Legal & Disclaimer

The information contained in this book and its contents is not designed to replace or take the place of any form of medical or professional advice; and is not meant to replace the need for independent medical, financial, legal or other professional advice or services, as may be required. The content and information in this book has been provided for educational and entertainment purposes only.

The content and information contained in this book has been compiled from sources deemed reliable, and it is accurate to the best of the Author's knowledge, information and belief. However, the Author cannot guarantee its accuracy and validity and cannot be held liable for any errors and/or omissions. Further, changes are periodically made to this book as and when needed.

Where appropriate and/or necessary, you must consult a professional (including but not limited to your doctor, attorney, financial advisor or such other professional advisor) before using any of the suggested remedies, techniques, or information in this book.

Upon using the contents and information contained in this book, you agree to hold harmless the Author from and against any damages, costs, and expenses, including any legal fees potentially resulting from the application of any of the information provided by this book. This disclaimer applies to any loss, damages or injury caused by the use and application, whether directly or indirectly, of any advice or information presented, whether for breach of contract, tort, negligence, personal injury, criminal intent, or under any other cause of action.

You agree to accept all risks of using the information presented inside this book.

You agree that by continuing to read this book, where appropriate and/or necessary, you shall consult a professional (including but not limited to your doctor, attorney, or financial advisor or such other advisor as needed) before using any of the suggested remedies, techniques, or information in this book.

Table of Contents

Introduction

When most of us think about chess, the foremost thought is the difficulty involved. Chess itself can be a very intimidating game for beginners. Still this is not an impossible game to learn. In fact, chess actually began in India as a courtly game of strategy. These games of strategy were used to help princes and generals learn to think outside of the box, a skill that would serve them well on the battlefield. Over time, chess began to be prized for the skill needed to win the game itself. Tournaments were organized. Men strived to have the title of chess master.

Kings would hire teachers for their sons and those who excelled were praised. Women were not taught chess, as it was considered a man's game for much of its history. Only within the last one hundred years or so have women too begun to pick up the pieces of chess, exploring the strategy and challenge that this game provides. Championships are held for a variety of groups, ages and backgrounds. While this is a game that started out for kings and nobles, it has become a game of the people at large.

In its earliest form in the 6th century, chess was based on early military divisions of the infantry, cavalry, elephantry and chariotry. Over time, these divisions evolved into what is known today as the pawn, bishop, knight and rook. The spread of chess followed trade routes, moving from Indian through the Middle East and China into Europe and Russia. By the 11th century, chess as game of both royalty and the wealthy had been intricately woven into society. Since that time, chess has evolved into the game of skill that we see today, whether it's in the park or in a tournament.

With such a rich history, chess has truly become part of the culture of both Eastern and Western societies. Instead of being intimidated, let's explore chess and all its amazing facets, starting with how this amazing game first began, in one of the cradles of civilization, India.

Chapter 1: An introduction to chess

The history of chess

In the earliest forms of chess, it was known as the game of four divisions, representing the military and its divisions. India received the game from the Persians, where it was part of a noble's education. As the rules developed, players would yell "King" or "The King Is Helpless!" two phrases that over time would turn into what we know today as check and checkmate.

Islam continued the spread of chess, with the pieces keeping the names originally assigned to them from the Persians. As time went on, chess spread throughout the world. By the 9th century, the game had reached Western Europe and Russia. Traders brought special chess pieces throughout their travels.

In fact, the first chess pieces documented in Western Europe came from Muslim traders. Variations popped up in various cultures, from Buddhism to China. In the Far East, the game was played on the intersections of the lines versus in the squares themselves.

Once chess had spread to Europe, it developed and took shape, becoming very similar to what we know as chess today. In the modern history of chess, rule and competitive play have become part of the game. Chess teams in high schools and colleges play for the honor and accolades of their school, even if there aren't as many individuals to cheer for them that understand the game.

Like any other game or sport, charismatic players have increased its popularity. But let's take a step back to India for a look at how chess was played in the 6th century.

In India, the earliest form of chess was called Chaturanga. This game had two features that survived into all other variations of chess, which was the different pieces having different powers and that declaring the winner depended on the fate on one piece. Today, that piece is the king.

Chess was designed to be played on an 8x8 squared board. This board was originally used for backgammon type race games and adapted to the game of chess. The name Chaturanga literally means four limbs or parts. These four parts, for the purpose of the game, comprised the parts of a military force in that time period, namely the elephants, horsemen, chariots and then the foot soldiers.

It is this tie to the military that had chess dubbed a game of military strategy, as those who played it most frequently were either commanders or kings, both of which would be charge of soldiers. Early forms of chess may have been played using a dice, which decided the piece that would be moved.

There is an unproved theory that chess itself started as a dice game but the gambling and dice were removed over religious objections, namely Hinduism, which is one of the primary religions in India. Still, that military background continued and chess was used a tool for strategy, gambling, mathematics and even some astronomy.

The chess pieces themselves were made of ivory, a material prevalent in India at the time. In some variants, wins could be made by virtue of a stalemate, where the king was the only piece left to your opponent.

Early chess moves were assigned by the piece. As a result, each piece could only be used in certain ways, but these moves varied from Persia, India and Southwest Asia.

The king has remained the dominate piece. The queen can move one square diagonally at a time.

With the bishop, the moves it could perform depending on the location where the game was being played. In Persia, the bishop could move two square diagonally, but could also jump over any piece in between. The Indian version said the bishop could move two squares sideways or front and back, but could also jump over a piece in between. Southeast Asia limited the bishop to only one square diagonally or one square forward. The knight and rook have the same abilities we see in modern chess, which we will cover later.

The pawn could move one square forward and capture one square diagonally forward, but must be promoted by the queen.

One of the earliest games was recorded from the 10th century between a historian and his pupil in Baghdad. In the 11th century, a raja visiting from India used a chessboard to explain past battles.

Chess pieces started out as elaborate pieces of art in themselves, depicting animals and other ornate pieces. In Islam, however, the pieces were assigned names and abstract shapes because Islam forbids the depiction of humans or animals in their art.

In China, the game was altered to where the pieces were placed on the intersections of lines and not within the squares themselves. The whole point was still the same as with the chess from Persia and India, which is to disable the king, rendering it helpless.

Sometime around 1200, the rules of chess began to change in southern Europe, with these changes forming the base of chess as we know it today. Pawns gained the ability to advance two squares on their first move. Additionally bishops and queens were given their modern moves. The stalemate rules were finalized in the early part of the 19th century. This form of chess became known as Western chess or international chess, distinguishing it from other versions, including historical ones.

As the game of chess evolved, theories began about the best ways to win. Clergymen developed various opening elements and they analyzed simple endgames. In the 18th century, the center of chess life moved to France. There were two French masters, one a musician named Francois-Andre Danican who discovered how important pawns were for strategy; another was Louis-Charles Mahe de La Bourdonnais, who won a series of chess matches with Alexander McDonnell, an Irish master. Coffee houses became centers of chess activities, especially in big European cities. These coffee house matches were the beginning of chess organization, such as chess clubs, books and journals. There were matches between cities even, thus beginning the birth of the sport of chess.

Birth of Organized Chess

Howard Stauton, an English chess player, organized one of the first modern tournaments back in 1851. London was abuzz when the winner, an unknown German named Adolf Anderssen. He was hailed for his energetic attacking style, typical of the time. Over time, the nature of chess became as much a source of debate as the game itself. The idea of anticipating attacks and then preparing for them became a scientific approach that attempted to create and exploit the weaknesses of your opponent.

Wilhelm Steinitz revolutionized the game by breaking down a position to its components. He created defenses and strategies that depended more on the other pieces, instead of simply striking quickly with the queen. In 1886, he was regarded as the first official World Chess Champion. He lost his title to a German mathematician Emanuel Lasker, who retained his title for 27 years and is widely hailed as one of the longest world champions in history.

Moving into the 20th century, the number of tournaments and annual matches grew. For example, in 1914, Tsar Nicholas II of Russia awarded the title of Grandmaster of Chess to five men, although it was disputed. The World Chess Federation was founded in Paris around 1924. The Women's World Chess Championship was founded in 1927. Throughout the world wars, chess continued to grow. New theories, such as the hyper modernists who believed in controlling the center of the board with distant people, inviting the opponents' pawns into the center and then attacking them.

After WWII, an era of Soviet dominance in the chess world occurred. American Bobby Fischer was the only champion that interrupted the Soviet dominance, until the end of the Soviet system of government. A system of matches was developed during this time period that allowed for the strongest players to be seeded into tournaments. From these tournaments, individuals would go to the chess version of the playoffs, gradually reducing their number until one was left. That one would play the reigning Champion for the title. If they won, the original Champion would be able to challenge them again in one year. Everything moved on a three year cycle, so a champion was crowned every third year.

These tournaments continue to this day, with the last one being held in 2013. But what was the effect of chess on the culture?

Chess was part of the culture of nobles during the Middle-Ages and the Renaissance. It was a teaching tool of war strategy and even morality. The chess pieces were used as metaphors for the various classes and the duties of individuals came from the rules of the game or the properties of the pieces themselves.

In the modern culture, chess became a means of self-improvement. Benjamin Franklin said it helped us to gain foresight, circumspection and caution, skills which are important in real life. This train of thought has continued to hold true to some degree, as the game of chess is taught in schools and tournaments have been created specifically to reach out to children.

Within the arts, chess itself has been depicted as a key to the greater story. Films such as Ingmar Bergman's The Seventh Seal use chess as key to the struggle of the two protagonists.

The chess board

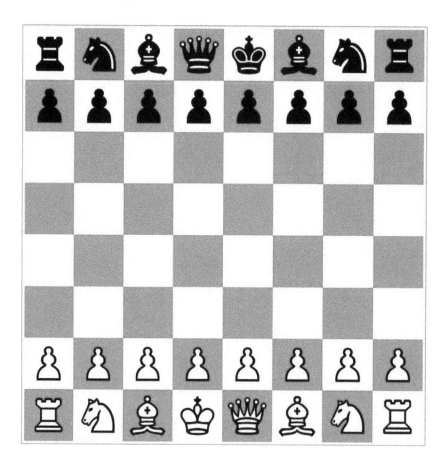

I know you might have seen a chessboard before – well, if you haven't, the image above shows a typical chessboard. It has all the chess pieces well arranged in their proper positions just before a game starts.

Notice that the board shown above has 64 boxes that are colored white and blue. Thirty-two of the squares are colored in white while the remaining thirty-two are colored in blue (in the image shown above). While the white color is standard in almost all chess boards, some chess boards have darker colors that range from red to black to green, etc. The most prevalent dark color used on the chessboard is black.

No matter the color used for the dark squares of the chessboard, the squares are often referred to as "dark" and "light." So, even if the darker color is brown or blue, the squares will still be called "dark" and "light." In this book, we'll follow standard practice and refer to the squares of the chessboard as "light" and "dark." The reason for this is that the darker squares or boxes can assume any color while the light squares can assume several shades of gray. For the chess pieces, we shall be referring to them as "black" and "white."

The chessboard and its coordinates

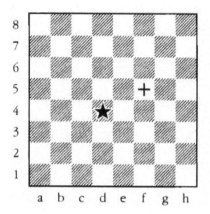

The image above shows a chessboard as a simple diagram with two coordinates.

If you look closely at the diagram, you will notice that the boxes or squares at the top left corner and those at the bottom right corner are lighter in color. The letters and numbers shown on the diagram are a coordinate system used to depict a particular position on the chessboard.

For instance, if I want to describe the position of the (+) in the chessboard above using the coordinate system. I would simply say that the (+) is sitting on the (f, 5) square. Alternatively, I can say that the (+) is sitting on "f5."

If I want to refer to the position of the star on the chessboard above, I can say that it is sitting on "d4" or (d, 4).

In chess, the normal convention or tradition is to highlight the board from the white piece's point of view. Remember, the player with the white pieces makes the first move. So, "white" normally plays up the board.

Ranks and files

You have probably heard the term "ranks and files" before, or you might have used it when making statements. Well, in chess, we also have what's called "ranks and files." For a proper explanation of certain ideas, maneuvers, and moves, names are given to different components of the chessboard.

For instance, the lines that move across the board either from left to right or right to left are called ranks. In the picture above, the line of squares or boxes where we have the stars is called the fourth rank. Notice that the stars are on the fourth line from the bottom of the board. If the stars were on the fifth line, for instance, we'd say that they are on the fifth rank.

In the same way, the lines that move from the bottom of the board up to the top are known as the files. In the second image shown above, the squares containing the stars are referred to as the d-file. While the line that holds the cross signs is known as the g-file.

Since you now know what ranks and files mean on the chessboard, we will now proceed to talk about what the sectors mean on the board.

Sectors of the chessboard

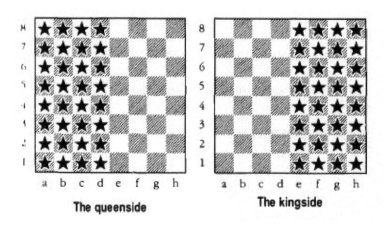

The queenside   The kingside

For the proper description of the different components of the board, the chessboard is divided into two halves or sectors. One sector of the board is called the kingside while the other sector or

21

half is known as the queenside. You will understand why they are so named when you get to a subsequent section of this book.

Remember, we often look at the chessboard from the "white," perspective. So, to describe the queenside, let's look at the first image shown above. The left side of the board shown above comprising of a-, b-,c-, and d-files make up the queenside.

The remaining right-hand side of the board comprising of e-, f-, g-, and h-files make up the kingside.

Square

If you have been playing chess for some time, or studied the openings in chess, you may have heard discussion about dark or light square weaknesses that one side is trying to capitalize on. What is going on when they say that, and what kind of moves are being discussed to take advantage of these positional elements? Generally, the strengths and weaknesses of a given position are determined by the pawn structure. When a pawn chain is formed, and a player is controlling the majority of one color with their pawns, they're said to have 'color dominance.'

However, it is important to note that having dominance in one color usually leaves a weakness in the other color squares.

Here are some key takeaways:

The most important part of determining light and dark color control is pawn structure.

If you plan to use a color dominance strategy, maintaining your weak color bishop is vital to your defense.

Focusing on a certain color square can overwhelm your opponent by creating instability in the position that you can take advantage of.

In the end-game, locking pawns onto squares opposite of your opponent's bishop is a great way to use this strategy to keep yourself safe, and make their bishop a "bad-bishop".

In closed positions with a strong focus on squares of a particular color, the knight can, oftentimes, find a great outpost in the weak squares your opponent leaves behind.

Find a meaningful way for an otherwise bad bishop to contribute. If you plan to lock in your pawns, try to free or trade-off that bishop before closing off the pawn chain.

Chapter 2: Getting to know the pieces and their powers

Explain all the pieces and their functions

The **King** is the most important piece in chess, but it's also one of the weakest. It can only move one square in any direction: forward, backward, sideways and diagonally.

The **Queen** is the strongest piece in the game. She can move in any direction just like the king, provided that she doesn't move through any of her own pieces. The queen's power combines the powers of the rook and the bishop. The queen cannot move like a knight. Like other pieces, if she captures an opponent's piece her move is considered to be over.

The **Rook** moves in a straight line in any direction: forward, backward and sideways. The rook cannot jump over any piece. It is a very powerful piece, especially when protecting other pieces of its own.

The **Bishop** moves along any distance diagonally as much as it wants as long as it doesn't jump over any pieces. Bishops on black squares will always remain on black squares while bishops on white squares will always remain on white squares. Bishops typically work well together because they can cover up the weaknesses of each other.

The most radically different piece in the chess army would be the **Knight**. The knight moves in an L-shaped pattern, moving one square up and two squares over or two squares up and one square over, two squares over and one square back, etc. The L-shaped pattern must be maintained in the knight's movement.

Pawns are positioned on the second rank of each player's army. White pawns start on rank 2 and black pawns start on rank 7. The first time a pawn is moved it can move forward either one or two squares. A pawn cannot jump over another piece. After it has moved once, whether moving up one or two squares, a pawn can only advance one square at a time. Pawns can never move backward. If a pawn advances to the end rank (rank 8 for white, rank 1 for black), then it will earn a promotion, meaning it can be exchanged for any other piece, except for a king or another pawn.

Relative Value of the Pieces

King – Infinite (Checkmate the king, you win the game.)

Queen – 9 Points

Rook – 5 Points

Bishop – 3 Points

Knight – 3 Points

Pawns – 1 Point

En Passant –From here, the other pawn has the ability to capture it as it passes by. This step has to be taken immediately after the first pawn has moved past. Otherwise the ability to capture becomes invalid.

How they move

Suppose all knowledge of chess can be gathered and united in one principle. How exciting will it be? Everyone wants the "final" principle to be understood, and each beat in chess with the possession of that expertise. Who could beat you? You have the final theory.

The bad news: there is no such hypothesis. It likely will not ever be one. However, Gary Danelishen has published whose book title itself suggests: "The Final Theory of Chess" The book explores precisely how this dilemma can be solved. What is the answer to this forever-evasive question, "What is the best move in the world?"

But is there the strongest movement in the world? I doubt that.

Foremost, the issue is just too broad. This broadness should be reduced to a certain specificity by another condition. This can be achieved by asking: "What is the best move in this position?" Here we have incorporated a new parameter - by being more precise (i.e., "in this position").

"If this happens, then that happens. Unfortunately, suppose this is the logic by which you work out a problem, even a mathematical problem. When asked for a solution, you can only conclude that the answer to the question is infinite. "If this happens, then that happens, and if that happens, then that one happens, then that, then that." ad infinitum.

What's the right thing to do then?

Attach a particular parameter. Before answering, "What is the best move in this position?" ask, "What position do I want to achieve?"

"This is the position I want to achieve; therefore, I go for this move." If you know what to do, you are apt to go that way. This reasoning can give a mathematically challenging impression of vagueness, but it's a wrong impression.

It also gives a sense of concreteness to the decision-maker. A certain target can determine a finite sequence of moves, even though the chess player's position estimation is based on subjective judgment.

Simple knowledge prevails over computation. If you know the factors, you can't calculate. Anything he doesn't know cannot be measured. This reality is obvious where the subject of knowledge is concerned. This is direct evidence: even the best players do not rely on pure estimation.

Viswanathan Anand, the world chess champion, is also an "intuitive" rather than a "calculating" player. Then there are many chess legends and other incredibly good modern chess players in history.

But what's all this saying? Danelishen writes in his novel,

The final theory of chess attempts to lay a sound basis for further study to achieve the first aim of a partial solution to the chess game. Day-by-day computer research was performed between mid-2004 and 2008, and Chess's Final Theory was slowly written.

The Fritz family of computer chess programs was measured around the clock by a network of six computers. Every previous analysis round provided the basis for future analysis."

However, the process is too slow (relative to the lifetime of the human person).

Ok, the underlying assumptions are:

1. There is an average of 40 legal moves from each board position.

2. A chess game takes an average of about 30 half-moves (60 or 60 half-moves).

There are, therefore, 40^60 (40 to 60 power or 40 times 60 by itself), which means 10^96 potential termination positions that must be verified by the machine.

If the machine can measure 10^18 final positions a second (actual computers aren't able to do so), 10^96 divided into 10^18 second positions will be 10^78 seconds or approximately 70 years.

Finally, discovering an 'end' theory of chess by finding the solution to all chess positions (in mathematics, known as 'brute-force calculation') is a practical impossibility. I find it more persistent in holding that the end theory of chess is this: there is no such thing as the final theory of chess."

Why Learn To Play Chess?

How many times has anything new been attempted, but soon it was difficult to learn? You know how easy it is to give up if you're like me. "That's too hard! Why do I?" I find myself asking, "That is too hard! Why do I do this?" Before I began, I didn't decide why I wanted to do it.

Recently, I have received this message: "Thank you very much for my download, but (chess) it's not an easy game to understand.

Here is my answer:

I accept that chess is difficult to master. There are also rules to remember. Each piece is going in a different direction. Every game is different. It is different. This is why I need strong reasons to learn how to play, or else I'll beat down and beat down again. Why then learn to play chess?

Since it teaches us lessons in daily life! Here are only three competencies we can build. There are, I'm sure, several more.

Chapter 3: The Rules and Chess Notation

"What are the rules of chess success?"

Many chess players around the world starting and improving are left scratching their heads and posing the question above.

They spend sleepless nights studying various Open Sicilian variants. They sink their heads into chess strategies and read thickness-like strategy books. You see videos of your favorite Grandmaster or chess teacher teaching one or two things about playing the game.

HOWEVER, despite the long hours spent in chess preparation, you do not produce the consistent results you like! These chess players will win beautifully and magically in a game, but they'd lose and crush like someone who played his first chess match against a master.

You're probably one of these players. You won't be here if you only win games, tournaments and compete at a prominent level

Well, don't worry. This chapter will outline basic rules that will help you improve your chess dramatically in 23 days!

1. Play chess sometimes.

This advice sounds simple, but trust me, that many players ignore this advice. They spend two to three hours practicing opening chess, medium game tactics, chess, etc. However, they can hardly find the time to play a competitive chess game or two in one week.

Chess is a sport of touch. The deeper you sink into it, the more complications and subtleties, you know but playing chess alone will not take you far.

2 Instructive analysis of game masters

Again, we have another golden piece of advice not considered by chess players in university. Many like "Winning With The Dilworth Attack," "Winning With The King's Gambit," etc.

If you want anything to succeed, you have to closely analyze the successful people in this industry and learn what they do. The same can be said for developing your chess. Look at how Mikhail Tal blasts his chess combinations into oblivion.

3. Please note: This is the most important rule and advice I offer here to advance chess, so keep your eyes glued.

Here is it: develop your chess thinking process and make it effective.

Chess is a thought game. We all know that. No amount of opening planning and memorization will benefit you. Your chess thought method - whether it's effective or not, will decide if you will come out on top or fall in defeat.

Learn how to think PROPERLY - this is the most critical rule of chess success!

If that's the case, then you can take advantage of an experienced chess coach and Grandmaster's straight forward, efficient thinking tools and clear-cut rules of chess performance! Know what the chess thought method should be made of.

A Simple Way to Understand Chess Notation

In chess games, the movements have been recorded for centuries. The way they did this is by a form called the chess notation. It is a straightforward way to write down every move to be registered and shared properly.

The alphabet is commonly used in chess notation as one side of the chessboard is written from a to h. The chess pieces are also represented with the letters of the alphabet. As the King is used, a K is displayed, and a Q is displayed. A different letter can be used for the Bishop, depending on the area. To represent the Bishop, France uses the letter F, and other countries use B.

Since the King is K, the Knight cannot use K, so it uses N. It's because of the nickname Knights, the rider at night. The Knight is also symbolized by an S, the initial letter for Knight of the German word. The rook is marked R, and every pawn is marked P.

PIECE	ENGLISH	FRANCE	GERMAN	ITALIAN
KING	K	R	K	R
QUEEN	Q	D	D	D
BISHOP	B	F	L	A
KNIGHT	N	C	S	C
ROOK	R	T	T	T
PAWN	P	P	B	P

The numbers used are from 1 to 8. Since there are 64 squares and the game is 8x8, it makes sense to use a combination of numbers and letters to decide the exact location of each piece with a simple and simple procedure.

At space a1, the left white rook is the point of departure for the notation scheme. This makes it much easier to write down the games than to explain in practice every move for and piece of chess. This allows each player to communicate their chess movements by e-mail, communication, or video and other means without seeing each other move.

Some players will have a chessboard for each player so they can visualize every player. In email chess, the player first takes the move and then sends the email. The other player doubles the same move and then prepares the next move.

The simulation process is maintained while players are in various positions by having a chessboard for each player. This is not important in video transmissions where each player can see the move for itself.

One player can send a mail (Nb1 to Nc3) telling the opponent where his knight will go from b1 to c3). Then he moves the piece of his Knight on his chessboard from b1 to c3. The opponent's player receives the email (Nb1 to Nc3) and places the Knight piece on the receiving board at c3. The chess player who receives then agrees on a counteraction or a new maneuver.

He will e-mail the first player with his move notation, then move to the chessboard. The game continues like that. The chess player will not change the movements of the chess piece by sending an e-mail first. If a player wants to move a chess piece, he will email and make the move.

When ready, the second chess player can call the first player's precise mode. This removes much incomprehension, and miscommunication and errors do not extend the chess game.

To develop your game, a notation will encourage you to disclose your weakest spots to understand what they are and reinforce them to strengthen your chess game. More accurate notation methods and explanations are available, but that is enough to start you.

A notation is a chess strategy used for illustrating pieces of movement on a chessboard without having a visual chessboard diagram for every move. It increases the chess writer's ability to define many compact chess games, which leaves more space for game analysis. It also helps the author, rather than needing hundreds and hundreds of complicated chessboard diagrams, to focus on chess strategies and tactics.

The name of the piece represents the movement, and then by a dash, and then by the name of the square it moves to. E.g., Q-QB8 means the queen moves to QB8 square. Square names are often simplified if it is apparent which square is identified. To define a knight, both "KT" and "N" are used.

Important notes: verify with "+" or "ch" is defined. A capture is labeled with an "x" followed by the captured piece. If the game is difficult and is not clear which part is listed, the explanation will often state whether the kingside or queenside part is moved.

The simpler definition will read QR-K7 instead of R-K7. P-K7=Q implies that the pawn moves to K7 then is elevated to a queen. Castling is called O-O or O-O-O.

The best way to familiarize yourself with descriptive notation is by going to my chess strategies page, scrolling down to the bottom, and clicking on a resource link. I have on that page chessboard diagrams listed and a sample game in descriptive notation along with simple chessboard diagrams so you can easily see which piece moves.

Chapter 4: Check, Checkmate and Draws

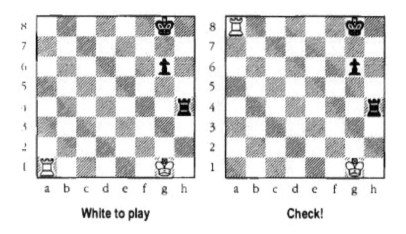

White to play   **Check!**

Look at the two diagrams closely and observe something. In the first diagram, let's assume that it is the turn of White to play, the rook can move from a1-square to a8-square. If that happens, as shown in the second diagram, it means that White is attacking the black king that is sitting on g8.

In chess, when an enemy piece attacks a king, it is referred to as "check." In the second diagram above, if Black wants to make a move, he is not allowed to make any other move apart from rescuing his king from danger. This can be done by using another piece to block the way between the king and the rook on a8. Alternatively, Black can move the king away from g8 to protect it from attack. In this chapter, we will be looking at the different ways of getting out of check.

Getting out of check by moving the king

In the check, you can see that the rook on a8 has placed the king on g8 in check. One of the best ways to protect the black king from this situation is to move it away so that the rook on a8 is no longer threatening it. If Black moves the king from g8 to g7, it means that the king has been moved out of check.

In the described above, are there other moves that would protect the king and keep out of check? The answer is no. In the out of check, if the king moves to f8 or h8, it would still be in check because the rook on a8 can still attack it. Of course, the king cannot move to f7 or h7 because there are two black pawns occupying those positions.

Getting out of check by capturing the checking piece

Apart from moving the king that is in check away from the threatening piece, you can also get out of check by capturing the checking piece.

The check depicts a game scenario that is almost similar to the one on the previous page. The only difference is that Black now has an extra piece – a black bishop that is sitting comfortably on d5. In the above scenario, the black king is also in check, and action must be taken to protect the king.

To get the black king out of check, one option would be to move the king from g8 to g7-square. A second valid option would be for the bishop on d5 to capture the checking rook on a8-square. If that happens, the rook is removed from the game, leading to the second diagram above. Since the checking piece is already out of the game, the king gets out of check. See the second diagram for clarification.

Getting out of check by blocking the line of fire

Apart from moving the king and capturing the checking piece, another viable way to get out of check is to block the line of fire.

Notice that the scenario in the diagrams above is similar to the previous ones we have seen earlier. However, the only addition is that this time around, Black has yet another bishop, sitting on b4. A white rook on a8 is also checking the king on g8.

As seen earlier, the king has the chance to move to g7 and be out of check. The black bishop can also capture the checking rook on a8 and replace it. Also, the second black bishop on b4 can move to f8 and block the line of fire, hence protecting the king from check.

You have now seen what check means and the different ways of getting out of check – we now want to look at checkmate and what it means.

Checkmate

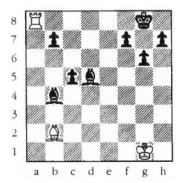

Checkmate happens when a king finds himself in a situation where he has no chance of getting out of check.

Look at the diagram above, it is a bit similar to the ones we have been using in this chapter, but with a few variations. There is a bishop on the b2-square. Again, the king on g8 is in check. As you can notice, if the king moves to g7 as it did in the previous scenarios, the bishop on b2, which moves diagonally, will become the king's new checking piece.

Notice also that Black cannot use the bishop on d5 to capture the white rook on a8, as was possible before – the reason being that there is a black pawn blocking the way on b7. Black cannot also block the line of fire using the bishop on b4 as there is a black pawn blocking the path on c5. So, there is no way the bishop on c5 will get to f8 to protect the king.

As can be seen in the scenario above, Black has no way of getting out of check – in chess, such a scenario is referred to as "checkmate," and it marks the end of a game. In the scenario above, White wins.

When playing chess, your aim is to checkmate your opponent's king. Once you have done it, the game is over, and you win.

Checkmate: the aim of the game

As said earlier, your aim during every game should be to checkmate your opponent's king – once you have achieved that, then you have won. How do you checkmate an opponent?

Look at the diagrams above – it is currently Whites turn to play. Since it is White's aim to checkmate and win, let's look at the various ways in which that could be achieved.

White has four likely ways to check Black's king. The white knight can easily move to either f6 or c7. In either of those positions, the rook will check the black king. The rook on h1 can also move to h8 and check the king. Lastly, the bishop on f5 can move to d7.

While the four different moves shown above will check the black king, the only one that will checkmate the king will be moving the rook to h8. The black king will not be able to move along the 8th file, the rook is checking the king on that file. If the black king moves to d7, the bishop on f5 will check the king. If the black king moves to e7, the white knight on d5 will check the king. So, the game shown is checkmate – white wins.

46

Is it a checkmate?

Look at the above scenario closely, does Black have a way out? Let's analyze. In the diagram above, the white queen was just moved to a8, thus checking the king. Can we call that a checkmate already? We will only know that if we consider the various ways that Black can get out of the situation.

As you can see, Black cannot move his king to h7, because there is an enemy bishop on d3 waiting to attack. If the black king moves anywhere along the 8th file, the white queen on a8 will still be checking the king. Can Black capture the checking queen? As can be seen in the diagram, Black doesn't have any piece that can do that. Can Black block the line of fire? Yes, Black can move the rook on e1 or the bishop on a4 to e8-square. So, the scenario above is not a checkmate.

Which check is checkmate?

Look at the diagram below and determine which check is checkmate.

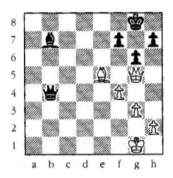

In the above diagram, it is Black's turn to play. What are the possible moves that Black can make to help him checkmate and win the game? Let's look at the various available options.

If Black decides to move his queen to either b6 or c5 to check the white king, White will either move his king to f1 or place his bishop on d4 to block the line of fire. If White moves his bishop to d4 and Black's queen is on c5, for instance, then White has the chance of losing his queen.

Now, if White decides to place his queen on b1, Black will easily move his king to f2. If you look closely, you will find out that if

Black moves his queen to e1, then White will have no other escape route. All escape routes like f1, h1, f2, and g3 are already being covered by black pieces. So it is checkmate and White wins.

Checkmate marks the end of the game

When people play chess, and their king is in check, they often try one last move to salvage the situation – they often try to take some actions against their enemy's king.

In the first diagram shown above, White checkmates black king by moving his knight to a6. Rather than acknowledging that the game is over, Black tries to throw one last punch by moving his knight to e2 in order to check White's king. In chess, this is not allowed. The game shown above has clearly been won by White. The first checkmate in a game ends the game.

The king may not be captured

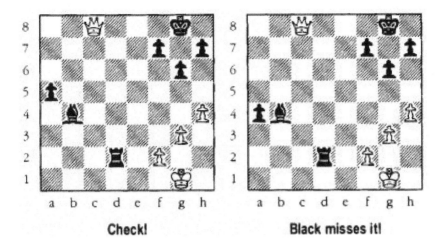

Check!　　　　　　　　　**Black misses it!**

In a game of chess, the king cannot be captured. Yes, you can check, and you can also checkmate the king, which marks the end of the game, but the king cannot be captured. This might sound like the opposite of what we have been saying all along.

However, when you check a king, the king is allowed to get out of the check. If you checkmate a king, the game ends; it doesn't go on one move further to make it possible for the king to be captured physically – this is why he is the king, by the way.

Even if a king is attacked and the king didn't get out of the check, you cannot capture the king. To understand this, look at the first diagram above. You can see that Black's king is currently attacked. However, instead of Black getting his king out of check, he forgets and moves his pawn from a5 to a4 rather. See the second diagram.

Despite the oversight, White cannot use his queen to capture the black king. What happens instead is that Black would be mandated to withdraw his last move – i.e., Black must return his pawn from a4 to a5. Next, Black will move his king out of check.

The position of the pieces on the board was quite similar to that of modern-day chess. However, the significant difference is the one that Shatranj inherited from Chaturanga. The pawn in Shatranj was also allowed to move just one square in their initial move while modern chess allows the pawn to move two squares. Another difference that was adopted from Chaturanga was the fact that the game ended once a player eliminated all their opponent's pieces, except the king. However, the stalemate rule was the opposite of what Chaturanga rules allowed. In Shatranj, the player who stalemated their opponent wins the game instead of the stalemated opponent, which was the case in Chaturanga.

During this period, several important players emerged. It was these players who recorded the first books on tactics and strategies. From these records rose the first archives of chess literature. These books were a testimony to the growth of chess and the experience of these players. Some of the well-known players of Shatranj who emerged at this time are As-Suli Al-Razi and Rabrab.

When the Arabs conquered Persia, they took Shatranj to the entire Muslim world. By the end of 1000 AD, the game traveled to Europe and Russia, where it became very popular. From there, it spread to China and Japan. With these travels, several variations were introduced to the game; most of which aren't seen today. Between the 13th and 15th centuries, the game underwent several changes. The rules were changed, and more tactics were discovered. Some of these rules are still seen in today's chess game. It was during this time that modern-day chess started taking shape. Most rules enforced during this period were to make sure that the game didn't take forever to complete, which is why pawns are allowed to move two squares instead of one. The concept of castling also came into existence during this time. It was also during this time that the Queen and Bishop got powers. There was a point when chess was referred to as the "Mad Queen Chess" because of the powers that were bestowed upon the queen. By the start of the 15th century, the game started looking more like the game we know today. This was when famous chess strategies and tactics came into play.

Chess Exciting Facts

Whether you play a wood chess set or a 21st-century electronic chess machine or maybe play virtual laptop video games, you play a charming and historical game. There are some cool things, approximately chess.

First of all, chess became probably about 5,000 years in the past in what originated in current India, and the primary chess recreation was perhaps the Indo-Chaturanga recreation. Chaturanga is a method in shape which took element on a tile or chessboard, much like chess, and the whole idea is to wonder the opponent's king.

However, Chaturanga may be played through 4 players simultaneously. "Ships" and "carriages" have been concerned, and the cube was used. One player did no longer start the in shape with an equal amount of portions as present-day chess. But the variations among Changer and Chaturanga are remarkably similar, likely the second model of the previous version.

The Arabs delivered chess to Europe and, once they did, seized the amazing Persian empire and spoke Persian within the equal way. The word "chess" from chess is derived from the Persian "chess-mat," which means "the king failed." Since chess is performed most effectively with nobles and very rich humans at the start and for centuries, it is referred to as the "King's Game."

The chess sports we recognize these days include medieval European society in competitions introduced using Arabs. At this time, the queen, the king, the bishop, the rook, and the knight have been invented based totally on Persian counterparts (the word "rook" is derived from the Arabic, meaning "car" - another evidence for the possible Chaturanga roots). However, the queen did now not emerge as the most substantial component at the chessboard till the Renaissance, and it turned into at this point that the infantry received the capacity to transport in squares at their first move. These rules had been made to speed up the game and create greater violations due to the fact the Rebirth was a rapidly converting duration in Fatah's thoughts. Renaissance queens additionally tended to be greater dependable than their medieval predecessors.

If you're into wood chess sets, because you love crafts and hand-carved traditions, you'll be interested in the chess units at Isle of Lewis - the oldest surviving chess inside the world, as anybody knows. Pedestrians seem like tombstones, and aristocrats appear to be in an awful, awful situation, and this suggests the unsightly attitude toward the arena that maximum people had when proper heads (pedestrians) generally have died at a younger age. 30 For their lives were very difficult. Pieces of walnut trunks are carved.

Whether you play in a wood chess set or an electronic chess set, you play math. Sixty-4 squares represent a sacred variety in historical India. The range of unique and unique chess video games to be performed is expected at a mind-blowing 10,120. The Dutch conquest of England mounted King Eschequer's Office of Collection and Accounting, naming his minister "Prime Minister Azkar." Because, at first, a checkered cloth covered the table, on which selections were issued. In historical French, the chessboard is translated as "counting desk," even as chess means "chess."

Chapter 5: Strategies

Opening Strategies

In the opening phase, strategies revolve mainly around the following goals

- developing pieces

- controlling the center

- keeping the king safe

- establishing pawn structure

Developing Pieces

Developing pieces entail bringing your pieces off their original squares to more useful positions where they can have maximum impact on the game. A player would normally bring the knights and the bishops out first, strategically moving the center pawns to unleash the bishops. Knights and bishops can open up attacking opportunities and help secure the center.

Develop the Knights Ahead of the Bishops. - Knights should be developed ahead of the Bishops. Knights are more useful if they are moved towards the center area where they can help control the four main squares. The opening is the phase of the game when you can position the Knight in optimal squares as there are only a few pieces out.

The Queen should not be taken out prematurely. Many novice chess players are easily awed by the all-powerful Queen and would consequently try to bring it out early in the game in the hope of gaining positional and material advantage. On the contrary, the Queen's special abilities are the very reasons why you should not expose your Queen in the early development stage. The queen should not be moved around much nor overused at this stage as this will make it more vulnerable prematurely. A threat on the Queen by an attacking piece will merely force you to move it to a safe square to avert early capture. It is smarter to develop your other pieces ahead and eliminate unnecessary threats or surprises from the opponent's minor pieces. You wouldn't want to have your Queen captured by the opponent's Bishop or Knight early.

Don't Move a Piece Twice in the Opening Stage. Your ability to develop each piece to its optimal square at the earliest time possible could very well spell the difference between success and failure in a game of chess. You should strive to develop all pieces rapidly. Moving the same piece twice in the opening phase unless really necessary is counterproductive and time-wasting. Developing all pieces is more important than launching attacks using one or two chess pieces.

While developing your pieces, try to make a move that will pose a threat to your opponent at the same time. While developing your pieces is a priority in the opening phase, introducing threats against your opponent while moving your pieces around is a good strategy to force him to take a defensive stance and disrupt the development on his end.

Focus on developing one or two pawns first. While it is important to develop your pieces early, this does not include advancing most or all of your pawns. Doing so will only weaken your defenses and allow your opponent's pieces to advance towards your King unimpeded. Ideally, you should focus on developing the pawns on the King and Queen's line to control the center and allow your pieces to develop well.

Controlling the Center

There are several good reasons why you should control the center. Control of the central squares – e4, d4, d5, and e5 – allows greater mobility when developing the pieces and allows your pieces better access to more areas on the board. When you move your Knight to a square near the center, for instance, you can easily expand its reach and usability. In the Middlegame going to the Endgame, most tactical maneuvers occur around the center. Hence, you can always expect a fierce battle to seize the center.

Since White makes the first move, it is generally considered that it enjoys a slight advantage. Black will of course strive to equalize and launch its own strategic attacks in the process.

Keeping the King Safe

Castling early is vital. While the game's objective is to force the opponent's King to submission, you should not lose sight of the fact that you and your opponent have the same objective. Develop your pieces in a way that prepares the path for castling in as little time as possible. The King's safety is crucial in all phases of the game and at this point, a properly timed castling is generally the best option to shield the King from dangerous possibilities. A weakened King's position can lead to a quick defeat or require a player to sacrifice other pieces. Hence, you should castle early.

Establishing Pawn Structure

You should try to avoid openings that create weaknesses on pawn structure such as pawn islands, doubled, isolated, or backward pawns. Some opening moves, in fact, are made to trap the opponent into overextending or forming weak pawn positions.

Middlegame Strategies

Many beginners concentrate on learning openings of chess too much, only to be disappointed if their opponents don't follow book movements. Others spend time researching the endgame only to discover they rarely arrive.

The Middlegame is most often ignored in chess but can help you make up for the lack of knowledge about openings and give you the edge in the endgame.

The Middlegame is normally the part of a chess game after the opening. For instance, when you move your job, bishops, and knights, the king has the sight of your rooks on the back row. Now you have a stable base on which your attack or defensive pieces can be placed if you choose.

Carefully placing the pieces to limit or compel your opponent to make a mistake gives you the advantage. This is where chess strategy comes in. You can practice Middlegame in chess by playing with a low skill level computer. You can either start the chess game from the start or, if you use a Fritz program, start from the end of the opening of chess from its database.

Now you should concentrate on a single chess square close King. Your goal is to either occupy this square or threaten it with at least two of your chess pieces, thus not permitting the enemy to strike or occupy the square simultaneously.

Work to ensure that no chess piece is left unprotected while moving the pieces and try not to be drawn by removing an opponent piece unnecessarily. This leads you to plan how you can maneuver your chess pieces with a certain target in mind.

You get over the habit of reacting with your enemies without considering a solid strategy.

The purpose of chess is to check the opponents' King, but many mini goals must be achieved before reaching this stage. This goal can also be accomplished in some ways, so chess strategy and tactics are so important. If we played in the same way every time, our chess game would be boring and easy to beat.

We must also adjust how we play. To accomplish this consciously, we need a strategy. It need not be complicated, but the method above lets you see how you can quickly and easily build these plans before any chess game.

When you learn how to manipulate a single square without distracting yourself, try to control the same but two squares on the chessboard. You can then control a square from which you can strike the king—controlling the chessboard in the endgame and a decisive advantage.

Endgame Strategies

The endgame is the phase when there are minimal pieces remaining on the board. At this stage, a pawn assumes a more prominent role as each player will strive to advance a pawn to the eighth rank and promote it to a more powerful piece. This is also the phase where the King takes a more active role in the game. A King takes the center board to attack opposing pawns, protect its pawns, and cramp the movement of the enemy King.

Here are Endgame strategies you can use to win your games:

Use your Rooks to restrict the movements of the opponent's King. The long range threat of a Rook is very effective in keeping the enemy King from protecting its Pawns or attacking your undefended Pawns.

Use your Rook to defend your Pawns and prevent the promotion of enemy Pawns.

If you have the advantage in material, simplify the board by exchanging pieces. As in the middlegame, you're not supposed to exchange your Pawns.

Escort a pawn to promotion. If there are opportunities to create a passed pawn, you should by all means clear the path for your Pawn.

The endgame is the perfect time to activate your King. You can use your King to attack undefended enemy pieces.

Coordinate your pieces before pushing your Pawns.

Push your pawns on both flanks.

While you can promote several Pawns to have multiple Queens, you should focus on taking advantage of any opportunity for a checkmate.

Essential Strategies

Following are the essential principles of chess:

• Do not make the mistake of moving the same piece twice in the beginning of the game

• Make sure to develop the Bishops after developing the Knights

• Queen Bishop should be developed after the development of both the Knights

• The development should be made across the board and not just in an area

• In the opening, do not take any of your pieces to the other side

- Make sure that your King is not filed once you are done with the castling

- Wait for the castling of the opponent before pinning the Knight

- Avoid trades that will help the development of opposition's pieces

- Avoid early attack on the opponent

<u>Space</u>

Different things being equivalent, the side that controls more space on the board has a bit of leeway. More space implies more alternatives, which can be misused both strategically and deliberately. A player who has all pieces created and no strategic deceives or promising long haul plan should attempt to discover a move that extends their impact, especially in the middle. In any case, in certain openings, one player acknowledges less space for a period, to set up a counterattack in the middlegame. This is one of the ideas driving hypermodern play.

The least demanding approach to pick up space is to drive the pawn skeleton forward. In any case, one must be mindful so as not to overstretch. On the off chance that the adversary prevails with regards to getting a secured piece behind foe lines, this piece can turn out to be such a significant issue, that a piece with a higher worth may must be traded for it. Larry Evans gives a technique for assessing space. The strategy (for each side) is to check the number of squares assaulted or involved on the rival's side of the board.

Control of the inside

The system comprises of setting pieces so they assault the focal four squares of the board. Be that as it may, a piece being set on a focal square doesn't really mean it controls the middle, e.g., a knight on a focal square doesn't assault any focal squares. On the other hand, a piece doesn't need to be on a focal square to control the middle. For instance, the bishop can control the inside from far off.

Control of the inside is commonly viewed as significant in light of the fact that strategic fights regularly happen around the focal squares, from where pieces can get to the majority of the board.

Focus control permits greater development and greater plausibility for assault and guard.

Chess openings attempt to control the middle while creating pieces. Hypermodern openings are those that control the middle with pieces from a remote place (for the most part the side, for example, with a fianchetto); the more seasoned Classical (or Modern) openings control it with pawns.

Activity

The activity has a place with the player who can make dangers that can't be disregarded, for example, checking the rival's above all else. They in this manner put their rival in the situation of utilizing their turns by reacting to dangers as opposed to making their own, preventing the improvement of their pieces. The player with the activity is commonly assaulting and the other player is commonly shielding.

Protecting pieces

It is critical to safeguard one's pieces regardless of whether they are not legitimately compromised. This helps prevent conceivable future battles from the rival. On the off chance that a safeguard must be included sometime in the future, this may cost a turn or even be unimaginable because of a fork or found assault. The methodology of continually protecting one's pieces has a forerunner in the hypothesis of Aron Nimzowitsch who alluded to it as "overprotection." Similarly, in the event that one spots undefended adversary pieces, one ought to quickly exploit those pieces' shortcoming.

Indeed, even a shielded piece can be helpless. In the event that the safeguarding piece is likewise guarding something different, it is called an exhausted piece, and will most likely be unable to satisfy its assignment. When there is more than one assaulting piece, the number of protectors should likewise be expanded, and their qualities considered. Notwithstanding protecting pieces, it is likewise regularly important to safeguard key squares, open documents, and the back position. These circumstances can undoubtedly happen if the pawn structure is frail.

Trading pieces

To trade pieces is to catch an antagonistic piece and afterward allow a piece of a similar value to be caught. As a general guideline, trading pieces facilitate the undertaking of the safeguard who regularly has less space to work in.

Trading pieces is typically alluring to a player with a current favorable position in material, since it brings the endgame closer and in this way leaves the rival with less capacity to recuperate ground. In the endgame, even a solitary pawn's favorable position might be definitive. Trading additionally benefits the player who is being assaulted, the player who controls less space, and the player with the better pawn structure.

When playing against more grounded players, numerous apprentices endeavor to continually trade pieces "to streamline matters". Regardless, more grounded players are frequently moderately more grounded in the endgame, though blunders are progressively basic during the more muddled middlegame.

Chapter 6: Speed chess

What you need to play

The exciting thing about speed chess is that it is a way to play a passionate chess game, even if time is limited and completes the lunch break. To play this chess game, you will need a chessboard and all the game pieces and a standard chess clock.

Rules

Another pleasant thing about this chess style is that you need not learn many rules. No International Chess norm rules have changed. The only difference is that you are at the mercy of the clock with your opponent.

Just a little catch is made for the rules; if one player's time is running out, their opponent must claim victory. If victory is not proclaimed verbally, then despite the time run out, the game continues.

How long do you spend?

If you can theoretically pick a time limit, the two most chosen periods are 3 to 5 minutes. This time makes the game more exciting, but it also increases the players' enthusiasm.

Who will play this game?

Just because you played chess lately, you shouldn't think you're ready for speed chess. True, 3-5 minutes seem to be a lot of time, but time runs in the middle of the game. You will not be ready for this game until you have played much chess and thoroughly know all the game rules.

The other thing you should think before you consent to a speed chess game is to demonstrate how players, who care about the game, and those who excel at the game, treat the Stanley Cup Finals like a professional hockey player. They love the game and spend all their free time playing. A good chess player excels at speed chess since they can almost immediately analyze and interpret the board.

If you play chess a while ago and feel like you know the game well enough, you can go online and play some pace chess practice rounds.

Improve In speed Chess With PROPER Time Management

Three factors will lead you to lose a chess game: (1) you have tested, (2) withdrawn, and (3) you have run out of time.

I don't know how you are, but here I see: to become a better chess player, you must learn how to treat the clock properly! Yes, it is vital you correct your mistakes and reach a higher understanding of how you play chess but don't forget that the timepiece is part of the game.

If you have an enormous material and position advantage or measure a forced mate in 5, it does not matter. If your clock dropped before you won, it's over. If you don't use your time nearly every game, you don't exercise proper time management.

Many chess players, even masters, make a mistake in time management in either way: (1) playing too fast (2) playing too slow (GM Reshevsky comes to mind quickly). Weaker players, most go too far, despite the time control of the chess game. It is linked to another issue with chess improvement - not a successful chess thought mechanism.

To improve in chess, you must learn how to think better to play chess better. Well, if you play too hard, you can't think, right! That doesn't allow you enough time to consider threats and push your opponents to move, the chessboard's overall position, the opportunities you have, etc.

Another form of inappropriate time management

Another form of unsuitable time regulation is wasting too much time on non-critical moves. It is not helpful to think for 20 minutes, which Knight you should create first. Knowing which of the two Knights will first be created won't help you win the game, but the time trouble in the game can cost you the point later!

Let me stress once again; the clock is a crucial part of our game. If you can't deal with that, can I recommend that you instead take up correspondence chess? Just kidding

Seriously, to learn how to control the clock, if you want to better chess and here are a few tips that should allow you to improve chess greatly:

(1) If you play too hard, it should GREATLY help you follow a good chess thinking method. HOWEVER, if you're like me, a perfectionist, you could play too slowly, which is a huge mistake. Read on. Read on.

(2) After each pass, write down your remaining time. This should allow you to be mindful of how you treat your time. NM Heisman advises that you compare the progress on the Board occasionally, perhaps in non-critical positions.

On the other hand, GM Smirnov advised you to look at your clock before pressing the clock (this is a smart way to make sure you do the tip above).

(3) Follow this improvement in chess and proper time management guidance on different time controls, and particularly slow games when combat is intense, and you can be tempted to play too slowly.

You can't expect chess to change without paying attention to the clock!

How to play

An increasingly common variant of the 'international standard chess is called speed chess. The play requires the use of a chess clock to calculate a certain period during which each player must move and automatically lose the game when the chess clock runs down on a player. Speed chess is not suitably recommended for experienced players with a detailed knowledge of the game, the etiquette, and the chess strategy.

Speed Chess comes from regular chess and is a convenient way to squeeze in a coffee break or anytime you have free time. All you need is a regular chessboard, a chess clock (with two clocks and the ability to stop each clock singularly while it is counted down), and a willing adversary. All standard chess rules are valid unless new rules to govern such quick play are overridden.

As opposed to international chess norms, an odd twist on speed chess rules is that both its competitors must watch the chess clock. When the clock expires, the active clock automatically wins, even though his victory depends on him, and if he does not notify, the game will continue until he is notified.

However, the clocks are above every place on the board, so even if a player had won a regular game, he would forfeit if his clock runs out. In speed chess, where a player moves illegally at any point in the game, whatever the chess's clock, the player again forfeits his opponent.

The chess clock can be set for 3 to 5 minutes in speed chess, although other timings are seldom used. It's a simple, engaging game, both exciting and inspiring to watch, which would probably attract more attention than a regular standard match.

In classical chess, too many speed games seem to make you impulsive. Experienced and experienced players typically can quickly switch from one-time control format to another, but novices and mid-level players must take care to play slow chess as described.

Although challenging, make a concentrated effort immediately after a blitz game to recognize crucial mistakes. Keep a diary and list at least some of your errors on the same day.

Gradually, a repetitive pattern of errors will appear that point to some of your chess' weaknesses. It couldn't see knight forks. By solving a few knight fork problems each day, the weakness will become a force-you can carry out a few complex forks on unconscious opponents!

Tactics in speed chess are of vital importance, and everybody knows how to develop tactical skills - to overcome many tactical problems. The key thing to note is to solve tactical problems directly in the novel.

This improves your visualization ability. Dejan Bojkov and Vladimir Georgiev's Chess Tactics course is the perfect course for tactics since it involves important aspects of the work of tactics and how each theme is detected in your games.

The versatility of games played is a key advantage of speed chess since you play so many more games covering many opportunities in a brief time. In speed games, endgame skills are necessary to turn the advantage into winning or to defend a poor position.

Besides thinking about errors in a blitz game, you can record it in a diary, which you can refer to later to learn in a good endgame book. A detailed reference book that clearly describes concepts is the Full Endgame Course by Silman.

A better understanding of each stage would improve your speed chess. Lars Bo Hansen's "How Chess Games Won and Lost" is a wonderful book covering all kinds of chess from the play in the middle to the endgames to creating a new repertoire.

Two crucial points must be remembered when playing pace chess. First, staying calm and concentrating on winning a 'healthy' game isn't easy with fleeting time controls. Two, you can't play on and on after one, especially if you're on a losing streak. This action, if it becomes a habit, is self-defeating.

Physical health is important to play all chess formats successfully. An exercise regimen in collaboration with a physician addresses all factors such as age, health, etc.

You must master the fundamentals of standard international chess before studying or playing speed chess as a separate individual. Many fundamental rules apply and allow you to control the different pieces and their uses. Speed chess is only recommended for the most experienced player because it needs quick and simple reactions to stop the chess clock.

It is also recommended that the rules that can easily be placed online are enforced to eliminate the potential for any disagreements that may result from this broad variation on the traditional chess game.

The best idea to improve speed chess is practice, and both your speed chess and your comprehension of the game will be strengthened quickly.

The days when two people sat across the chessboard, waiting for the other person to make a move are far behind us. Speed chess is becoming increasingly common in these fast-paced times. Until speed chess was introduced, a person could take their next move all day to deliberate.

Speed chess is paced; if a player reaches the preset time to pass, the whole game is immediately lost. If you are an inexperienced chess player, probably stay away from this game, at least for the time being. The chess players who excel in this chess have gained a profound understanding of the mark and game strategy

The best thing about speed chess is that it's a way to play a lively chess game, even though there is just limited time. To play this type of chess, you need a chessboard and all the game pieces and a standard chess clock.

The perfect strategy for speed chess

Often our abilities wither in the absence of the right direction. As they don't know how to rinse this talented plant properly, it gets dry. Note that chess requires your unwavering commitment, like every other discipline. Normally, young boys don't know how to use their free time, particularly those with potential. Follow the directions and become a good chess player.

1. Learn books about chess and magazines

After some play, read the book attentively. Play additional games and read the novel. You digest those points that seemed elusive or did not grip you every time. The best way to become a better player is not to play opponents but to play well-noted games. Typically cover one side of the winner's pass) and think about each move before looking.

To develop your game easily, type the moves of all your games, not just the competitive one which needs recording). It is better to write it in chess scorebooks since loose scoreboards can be lost quickly. Then play every game and make critical remarks. This is how the Grandmaster developed his chess skills and became professional without coaching in a brief time.

It would also be beneficial to read chess books by regular authors. Try to follow the notes in a specific style. If you get the old books where the notes are not algebraic, try to convert them into that form.

Even this exercise would give you a good glimpse of the complexities of the game. Write them down in a separate exercise book and do the same thing in mathematics to develop your ability. This exercise is enlightening.

Keep a small chess board with pieces and turn descriptive notes into algebraic notes. It is important since just a few years ago, the algebraic notation was conceived while the first chess-books were written in a descriptive style. Recall that it's not an exercise that takes time and time, but a very gratifying one.

Besides, some nice magazines or newspapers with chess columns read this. There is hardly any decent newspaper or newspaper today without chess columns. Learn and solve these problems. Your goal should be to prove the solution you have given is incorrect!

You should try to attack the issue individually. If you produce some other approach, you think you are in your chess studies' right direction. You can enter a club with a chess facility. You could develop chess skills with the other students.

Without thinking about changes, you will enjoy chess. This, however, is a natural tendency for an awakened mind to improve its output in any area. By following the methods recommended here, everyone can usually become a strong player in a fraction of the time.

Dr. Emanual Lasker (World Champion 1897-1921) considered that, given a rational approach, an average person would not have to spend over 200 hours in chess to reach a point where a master player would lose his or her handicap. Lasker's 200 hours were underestimated, but in months most players will certainly achieve a level that usually takes years.

Some journals publish daily chess columns featuring composed chess problems. An artificial position is a set-up in a problem. A solver is expected to find a means of the testing mat in several movements, normally 2 or 3, regardless of what the defendant responds. In these, White often makes the first (key step for uniformity. Only the main move is required in 2-move problems.

In 3-move problems, the second moves for the right solutions are needed. As the composer's goal is to make the job difficult, the main move likely will not take place in a real game for a player and will never be taken (except a Pawn) and never tested.

2. Play Senior Players Handicap Chess

Another form of handicap with chess clocks is possible. The specialist will play in a short period, with his adversaries much larger. If the skill gap is not too great, this handicap is better since the starting position is not adjusted. If the gap in capacity is high, using both systems is a clever idea.

You can't use a time handicap for individual games unless you have chess clocks. In simultaneous exhibits, however, a time handicap automatically functions. The expert steps from board to board and takes each move. The expert can only take a fraction of the time that opponents take, as the master can make 10,20,30,40 or more movements during one move by each opponent.

Since time immemorial, concurrent exhibitions have been an excellent opportunity for many players to oppose a master under conditions that offer amateurs a chance to win.

3. Have tools for chess

Playing chess with a well-programmed machine often adds to your abilities in chess. In our age of electronics, inevitably, chess would draw the attention of computer technologists.

The real revolution was sparked by small, cheap micro-computers in computer chess. The new models feature up to sixty-four levels of playing, programmed openings, and games, a voice that communicates moves and sensitized places to remove the need for a keypad. Most can play a reasonable game, while the more advanced models can play in open tournaments successfully.

As suggested, microcomputers are most beneficial to players who encounter an opponent with a challenge—level of teaching with programmed changes in opening and thus recommend the best actions to benefit students. Computers for top players are an effortless way to store knowledge about opportunities and end games. Most top players use personal computers.

4. General Advice

Ideally start playing with another beginner when you know the movements. Do not be discouraged if you remember the rules slowly. You will be habituated to the pieces' moves with a little practice and figure things out without remembering how anyone moves and catches them.

Chess is competitive, and the greatest incentive is a willingness to win. That's why you should play with another novice. You've got a chance to beat. It would be safer if you had an instructor who could supervise the game and govern the rules, and to point out where you went wrong during the game.

The textbook on all aspects of the game in one volume differs in size and price. Champions write some chess handbooks; chess teachers write others - they all help the beginner deeper into chess mysteries. Then anyone who wants to develop skills more will specialize by learning different aspects of the game, and there is a wide variety of aids.

Opening books range from lengthy manuals in many large volumes, not recommended for beginners, to books that describe why openings are played. The middle game is discussed by describing the underlying strategic concepts and providing examples of tactical combinations. There are many books on this topic.

The end game is part of the game that should be learned by all aspiring players. Here again, there are many books to choose from. Primary books are the best for beginners, describing universal concepts that will most likely arise. There are books for experienced players dealing with unique endings. Finally, we come to pick great players' games. We recommend books with detailed comments, especially for beginners.

Young learners are advised not to rely heavily on chess problems in this game to achieve mastery. These questions are as far from literature as crossword puzzles. They bone the strength of one's movement visualization.

Play many real games and overcome the issue of chess to keep your mind alert. Recall that in chess (the actual game), the game's goal is to beat the adversary who does not matter how this end is accomplished or how time is taken.

However, the adversary reflects the time in problems. The mate must succeed with the number of moves listed. Since the position in the problem is often quzotic, most experienced chess players then reject it as unacceptable.

But the problem-makers maintain that game requires an unnecessarily laborious and profitable wood move. The fifty games can be merged into one artificial role. Nevertheless, the best courses for young students are open to the wise combination of the two.

Chapter 7: Hitting the computer chess

The basic idea is that the computer will look at various possible moves and the opponents reply and then it's next move and so on up to a certain point. Next it will rate each resulting position (called a leaf evaluation) with a numerical score, and simply choose the move that seems to lead to the highest scored positions. It should be noted that almost all programs will think when it is not their turn, this is called pondering and is often an option that may be turned on or off in commercial software. There are essentially two ways of doing the move selection. The brute force approach, and the selective analysis approach.

The brute force approach looks at all of the possible moves in a position up to a certain depth. In some ways this is the easier way to program and debug a computer to play chess. Just look at every move and pick one. The problem is that chess is so complicated that when using this approach looking just a few moves ahead results in a huge (really huge) number of possibilities. This caused early chess computers to play very slow, and as a result of not being able to see far ahead, quite badly.

Humans play chess very differently. We look at a position and drawing on our experience quickly eliminate most moves from consideration. Then we can focus our time examining only the best (or so we hope) moves to decide which one to play. For example if during a chess game there is a trade of queens. Your opponent captures your queen with his, you pretty much know to take his queen back in return. You might look at not recapturing if you had a raging mating attack going, but you certainly wouldn't consider some minor pawn move on the edge of the board somewhere.

So programmers started using this type of search for their machines which is called "Heuristics". Standard chess knowledge like that a bishop pair is often better than a bishop and a knight, or that isolated pawns tend to be weak, were worked into the calculation. The strong program "Crafty" has made some of it's search criteria public. Here is the list.

Bishops of Opposite Color

Bishop Pair

Centralization

Development

Developing minor pieces before the Queen

Doubled Pawns

Doubled Rooks

Isolated and Backward pawns

King Safety

Knight/Bishop Outposts

Material

Passed Pawns

Pawns on same color as a single Bishop

Rooks behind passed pawns

Rooks on Open Files

Rooks on the 7th Rank

Trapped Bishops

Trapped Rooks

Various end game related advantages

Weak Back Rank

Most modern programs also include many other principles to guide their own play. These are usually closely guarded secrets. By using a selective pruning method computers became much stronger and much faster. The danger of this search method is that it becomes possible to overlook a move that violates the common guidelines of good chess play, but may be the perfect exception in an exact situation. Maybe in a certain position a move that violates the principals turns out to be great several moves later, but the computer "prunes" that move and never looks at it deep enough to see the benefit later.

As computers became faster with newer technology there was a shift back to the brute force approach, or at least a modified version. A modern home computer is so fast that they really can look at a huge number of moves, which let's the computer do what it does best, crunch the numbers.

Deep Blue was much less selective that most software for home computers because it had the processing power to just try and look at everything. This is why when you see a rating for a chess engine it will usually tell you what processor the rating was achieved on. The faster the computer the stronger the program running on it will play.

I should also mention that the program interface and the engine often can be changed. You can run the Fritz software interface (the graphics and controls) and have it use the Crafty engine to make it's moves for example. So if you download chess engines they often need another program to actual be able to have a graphic chess board to play on.

Some other features that chess computers use are opening books and tablebases.

An opening book is a set of opening moves that the computer has stored permanently to use at the start of the game. Do you remember what the 15th move in the main line of the Sicilian Dragon opening is? Your computer does! Once it no longer has "book moves" to play it will start it's regular search. When playing a computer you can usually tell when it goes out of it's opening book as it will stop moving instantly and slow down a bit. Strong modern computers will try to play opening lines that steer the game into the types of positions that computers are good at.

Tablebases could also be called endgame databases. They are a set of 100% worked out endgame positions. For example one notorious ending is bishop and knight against a lone king. This is a win but is difficult to do. A chess program that has that tablebase installed will play that position perfectly and virtually instantly. It is not figuring out how to win the position it is just reading the instructions of what exact move to play. Tablebases exist for all five piece or less endings. All six piece endings except for five various pieces against a lone king (which the program can win anyway) also exist. While helpful for playing the ending itself the real benefit of tablebases for a program is that they can quickly and correctly judge which endings to allow and which not to. This can be a nice advantage when calculating middle-game positions.

So now that we know how computers play chess, let's take a look at strengths and weaknesses.

What computers do well

They can search a lot of moves really fast and thus see very deep. Remember from the history section that Deep Blue searched 200 million positions per second. Even much slower computers are still very impressive. Pocket Fritz running on a mobile phone once earned a performance rating of 2898 in a tournament.

Computers can also move super fast. Let me tell you a little story. I once had a friend who loved to challenge people to play one minute chess with him for a dollar. He almost never lost. After watching him play for a while I discovered his secret. When both players became very low on time (which always happens in 1 minute chess) he would only move pieces right next to the chess clock so that he didn't waste time reaching across the board to hit his clock. Then he would win on time when his opponent reached which took a fraction longer. Well computers don't need to click a mouse or physically move anything, and so can move instantly. They also know when to claim a draw. They know if a position has been repeated three times, or if the 50 moves rule draw can be claimed.

The computer doesn't get distracted. Remember that silly song about the pinball wizard by the Who? He won because he didn't get distracted by flashing lights and buzzers. Well the computer doesn't get distracted by phone calls, doorbells and cats jumping on them. They don't get tired or hungry or need to go to the restroom. Most programs will let you pause the game, but that steadiness can be a huge factor in the machine's favor.

They don't blunder. The machine can get outplayed and forced into losing material but it won't simply hang a piece for nothing. If a computer gives you something for free look again, it is not as free as you think. Here is a game I played against Chessmaster 9000. I was playing white versus the personality called Buck who is 2361 rated.

Eric – Buck 2361 (Chessmaster 9000)

1.d4 Nf6 2.Nf3 d5 3.Bf4 Nc6 4.e3 Nh5 5.Bg5 h6 6.Bh4 Rb8 7.Ne5

Nxe5 8.Qxh5 Nc6 9.c3 g5 10.Bxg5

It seems like Chessmaster just lost the pawn on g5 for nothing, so I took it.

Rg8 11.Bf4 e5

Now it shows the point of losing the g5 pawn. The threat is Bg4 trapping my queen. My bishop is attacked and so is my queen.

What computers do poorly (or used to anyway)

The "horizon effect" is when a computer sees the loss of a large amount of material and will throw away other lesser material.

This happened a lot in the early days as the computers could only see a few moves ahead. By adding another move or two (losing a small amount of material) it would push the loss greater material over the horizon of it's sight. Thus not realizing that it will still endure the original loss.

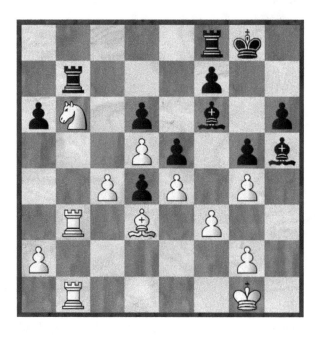

Some weaker programs are vulnerable to getting pieces trapped.

It's easy for a human to see that Bh5 was no good since g4 locks it out of play for a very long time. Computers can have a hard time understanding how bad it really is if it just counts the material and thinks all is still even.

Computers often have trouble with quiet positions where long range strategy is more important than tactics. If they can't see a clear result at the end of their search, they often mis-evaluate those positions. Things like which pawn structure is better than another can be difficult for a program if there are no clear answers to be found by calculation. Strong humans player can feel this sort of thing from experience.

Zugzwang is the concept that a position is OK now but becomes worse with any move. As players can't pass they must move and worsen their position. Computers sometimes have trouble with that concept as everything is OK at the moment. This comes up most often in king and pawn endings, which may be covered by a tablebase, but weaker programs or software set on lower levels often mess up fairly simple endings because of that weakness

Chapter 8: 17 Cool Facts about Chess(including the best players, kids and chess, different chess games)

Billions of Probabilities

For the first four steps in the game of chess, the number of possible variations of games is around 319 billion. This is, to say the very least, an incredible figure! In literature, no game can even equate.

Rookies

1st-year chess players are referred to as rookies, which is what we all call current military recruits, security departments, athletic teams, etc. The name derives from the last pawns in a chess match known as 'rooks' to pass.

The first-ever to beat a Soviet competitor in a foreign chess match back in 1924 in New York City was an American guy called Frank Marshall. For around 30 years, he was the existing United States leader and retained his championship when in 1923, he beat Ed Lasker. He was the first chess player to concurrently play more than 100 games.

Mechanical Clock

Thomas Wilson developed the first electronic clock to be used as a counter (rather than a sand glass back in 1883 in England. It was regarded as the chess clock 'tumbling'. A seesaw beam, it composed of two synchronized clocks. It stopped as one was turned downwards when the other clock began.

Fool's Mate Runs

The required number of moves is two to reach a checkmate, which is known as 'Fool's Mate Runs' or 'Two-Move Checkmate'. Black can only do this with the Queen on step 2, which is the lowest amount of moves necessary in a single game from beginning to end.

Youngest Champion

In 1985, the Soviet Union's Garry Kasparov (a journalist, community activist and chess player) had become the youngest global chess grandmaster to date. At the moment, he was just 22 years old. He is also called the greatest player of all time in chess!

King's Game

In India, where it arose, chess was originally regarded as the 'Game of Kings' because it was originally played by rulers generations ago. In the 12th century, the sport was a popular pastime for monarchs and rulers and also called its playing parts (pawns) after formal or worthy roles, like a king, knight, bishop, and Queen.

First Computer Chess Program

In 1951, the very first computer software to play chess was developed by Alan Turing. At the time, no machine was sufficiently sophisticated to analyze it, so Turing tried it himself, doing hand calculations and then performing each step according to the findings. This required considerable time on his part and extreme commitment.

Blindfolded Chess

Blindfolded chess is an outstanding ability held by the majority of good players. It needs the capacity to see the board directly through the mind, which becomes quite challenging after several steps. When playing around 50 games concurrently, several grandmasters have produced remarkable performance.

'Checkmate'

The term 'checkmate' derives from the Arabic term' shah mat,' which in English means' the King is killed (helpless).' "Real chess players do not say "checkmate" to an enemy, but rather stretch their hand, shake and say "nice game.

The Longest Possible Game

Based on the different movement variations, the longest game of chess will last around 5,900 passes. Without a player declaring a tie, this is the maximum number of movements that a game will precede. About 1,000 separate opening options alone are available!

Longest Reign as a World Champion

For the longest period, a German physician by the name of Emanuel Lasker claimed the position of World Chess Champion, from 1894 to 1920, for around 27 years. In modern history, this is the longest reign by a formally recognized chess master!

The First Space Game

In June 1970, the very first game to ever have been launched in space was chess. The Soyez-9 team played against their ground controls (astronauts Vitaly Sevastyanov and Andrian Nikolayev) and made nationwide news. Thought the game resulted in a tie.

The Longest Game Ever

In modern history, the longest chess game lasted for 269 steps (but finished in a tie). The longest game that is technically feasible is 5,949 moves, as described above. This will take forever to conclude, as the typical game lasts 38 moves and requires 10 to 60 minutes to play everywhere

The First Folding Chess Board

The very first folding chess panel was constructed out of desperation by a priest in the 12th century. The priest disguised his board by having it seem like two books put side-by-side because playing chess was prohibited by the church at the time.

Epic Fail

A Scottish-Canadian called Nicholas McLeod of Quebec, who defeated 31 matches in the double-round robin in New York in 1889, actually owns the worst results record by a professional chess player! At the peak of his chess profession in 1892, he was also the first opponent to defeat Emanuel Lasker.

The 2nd Book in English was on the chess

The second historical book to be written in English was all about chess. In 1474, 2 years before Jean de Vignay released it in French, William Caxton interpreted (and then published) it from French into English.

Most Versatile Chess Master

A man from India called Vishwanathan Anand seems to be the only chess player to claim the championship title in all three forms, namely knockouts, tournaments, and matches. Later, Norway's Magnus Carlson will move on to beat Anand in 2013.

Deep Thought

In November 1988, in Long Beach, California, a machine known as 'Deep Thought' became the first of its type to defeat a global champion in chess. Feng-Hsiung Hsu invented it and built it at the University of Carnegie Mellon. At IBM, it was later enhanced.

Teaching Chess to Children

An intriguing part of chess is that it tends to be played similarly well by teenagers and seniors the same. Broadly, Bobby Fischer shot to fame at a young age and even played a game touted as "the round of the century" at age 13. There are numerous ideas however that little youngsters discover hard to handle including the outcome of activity, strategies and thinking a few pushes forward. Fortunately however these abilities discover their way into the game naturally with training and time. In the same manner as other things in everyday life, if chess is found out early it will remain entrained in the memory of the player and will just proceed to advance and develop. Learning chess can be a long and difficult undertaking for some youngsters and along these lines to upgrade the degree of success, chess ought to be instructed gradually and must (and I mean must) stay fun and energizing consistently. The rest of this article is given to clarifying attempted and tried approaches used to show chess in stages by dynamically presenting piece acknowledgment, board setup, piece development, piece catch lastly chess itself.

The point of the game is to just pick a piece, yell its name and move the piece to an abandoned square anyplace on the chessboard. The game begins with the board designed as though you were going to play a round of chess. Players alternate in turns. Pieces are expelled from the board (caught) when they are encompassed by at least two rival pieces on neighboring squares. In the event that a player moves out of turn, erroneously names a piece or plays a rival's piece, the move is relinquished and the piece is returned. The game is won when the king is taken, or the king is the main piece remaining. This basic game has barely any principles but requires thinking ahead and basic procedure. For instance, pieces might be securely caught by first setting a watchman piece. The presentation of the procedure is by plan as the kid will dynamically understand that some methodology is required. This game is intended to show piece acknowledgment, alternating, the idea of catching and basic methodology.

When the kid is comfortable with Shout Chess, present a method for picking the player to move first by at first playing a brisk round of Speed Board. Speed Board basically includes the demonstration of taking one go each to arrangement the chessboard as fast as could be expected under the circumstances. While one player designs the load up the other player checks 60.The victor is the player who arranges the load up at all conceivable time or was not the player who neglected to design the load up inside 60 seconds. The champ of this esteemed game will have the pleasure of moving first in the following round of Shout Chess.

The following variety of Shout Chess might be presented after the child is unquestionably acquainted with the principles of Shout Chess. This variety acquires all the past rules of Shout Chess with the special case that pieces can never again be put anyplace on the chessboard, yet should now rather move according to the standards of ordinary chess. Contingent on the age of your kid, you may need to present this standard continuously by first enabling pieces to bounce one another or move just like a bishop or a rook. Gradually present the moves of each piece and at last end by showing your kid that knights are the main piece that can hop and that the pawn can move two squares on the primary move. This is the most confounded advance in the learning procedure and care should accordingly take to guarantee your kid appreciates this stage. Measure your youngster's delight levels and moderate the presentation of new moves if the fun factor lessens. Persistence and tirelessness are vital necessities.

The last stage is to present the ideas of piece catch, check and checkmate. Now, your kid ought to completely comprehend capturing a piece. Here we change the guidelines of Shout Chess by clarifying that you never again need to encompass a piece to catch it, however rather thump them off the board when you arrive on a similar square as them. We may likewise expel the obligatory prerequisite to yell the name of each piece as it is played and may even begin calling the game chess. Hold up a couple of matches before clarifying the corner to corner catch rule of pawns. Clarify check as a notice that your king might be caught on the following turn. Assurance of the king is a vital piece of Shout Chess and thusly ought not be an outside idea to your youngster. In the long run present the further developed ideas of castling, pawn advancement and en passant as your youngster's certainty levels grow.

There are boundless moves in chess, each relying upon the techniques of the rival. The openings or the principal moves a significant piece of the game, as are the remainder of the moves. At the point when one piece comes in the method for another, it is expelled from the board. Every player needs to secure his/her pieces and furthermore plan to dispose of the king of the rival. At the point when the king is killed, the game is finished. Notwithstanding, the game can likewise end in a draw, with neither one of the players overcoming the other.

There are numerous varieties in chess: rush chess (planned by a chess clock), shot chess/helping chess (exceptionally quick); correspondence chess (via mail), PC chess (played with the PC) and internet chess/online chess (played online with another player or the PC).

111

Now, your youngster is ready to comprehend the standards of chess, and can play chess at a fundamental level. Utilizing steady strategies will ensure everyone has a wonderful time and your kid will in this manner appreciate the learning procedure.

The Great Benefits of Introducing Chess to Children

The honorable craft of chess has gotten very prevalent with guardians with regards to teaching their youngsters about the different standards of life. These days, there are numerous guardians who find that the round of chess loans itself preferably to be utilized as an encouraging device for what they need their children to learn. Despite the fact that playing chess energizes a lot of fixation and connection, the best part about utilizing chess as an encouraging technique is that youngsters think that it's amusing to play.

Naturally, youngsters are exceptionally aggressive so playing chess isn't something that they will abandon effectively. They don't should be physically solid or particularly talented rationally, they just need to realize how to play the game and play it well. Kids love difficulties and this trademark in itself looks good for their accomplishment in the game.

The earth wherein chess is played acquaints youngsters with a lot of control; they figure out how to take on the difficulties that life can bring, and how to be benevolent washouts and charitable champs. Another extraordinary advantage picked up from being presented to the chess playing condition, is that kids likewise create social abilities and set up innovative approaches to help others. By and large, playing chess enables them to rehearse valuable fundamental abilities in the early piece of their lives, which is ideal for making solid mental aptitudes for when they get more seasoned.

Partaking in a professional workplace, maybe speaking to their school or school in rivalry, likewise sharpens fundamental ability characteristics that will help them in their later years. Coupling with others will assist them with supporting awareness of other's expectations and a minding soul. Helping other people gain proficiency with the game likewise empowers a merciful soul and a feeling of network in your youngster.

Another rule that youngsters learn, while playing chess socially, is that offspring of different sexes races and ages, ought to be treated with shared regard. They comprehend that when they are reasonable and kind to other people, it is generally responded. Contradicting this, they additionally find the negative impacts of treating others in an incorrect manner.

From playing chess, youngsters regularly find out about the estimation of diligent work. They find that nothing that is advantageous in life comes without diligent work and that apathy is a major "no-no". They perceive the estimation of steadiness, never surrendering, and develop significant qualities required for accomplishment throughout everyday life.

With regard to showing fundamental abilities, the round of chess is a brilliant instrument to help you in your child rearing endeavors. Playing chess will open your kid to new frames of mind and capacities that will place them at the cutting edge throughout everyday life and give them a strong establishment so they may impart their insight to their companions just as their kids and their kids' youngsters. The aptitudes that youngsters gain from playing chess are likewise the abilities that will place them in an advantageous position when they approach adulthood. It is difficult to think about a prepackaged game more valuable in this regard than chess.

Conclusion

When it comes to chess, strategy is the name of the game. Throughout the whole game, one is continually evaluating moves, both for their short term benefits and long term place within your overall strategy. From the opening to the endgame, the strategic plan is what helps you to beat your opponent, allowing you to create a checkmate.

This game doesn't just provide the strategic mental stimulation, it also has a long history dating back to before the 6th century. As a part of the social fabric of many cultures, it has stood the test of time, tying together humanity with a game of strategy.

Over the years, chess has now become a game of skill and tactics, with a variety of options, positions and rules of play. With international tournaments and other opportunities for the best of the best to play each other and test their skills, this truly is a global game of strategy. We have learned how chess is played in three phases and what each of the pieces mean in terms of position and ability.

The various opening moves and tactics, along with strong middlegame evaluations and endgame follow through can get you to a win. But along the way, you have to use a plan and follow it to the end. No plan when playing chess putting you into a position of weakness with your opponent or a sound plan can put you in a position of strength. While you have to react to your opponent's moves, remember they are also attempting to execute their plan to a successful conclusion. To get that checkmate, you just have to execute yours better!